CONTENTS

POP ICONS™ ANNUAL 2012

Published By Century Books Limted,
Unit I, Upside Station Building,
Solsbro Road, Torquay, Devon, TQ2 6FD.
books@centurybooksltd.co.uk   Published 2011.

TAKE...
FIVE

...TALENTED, HANDSOME AND HARD-WORKING LADS FROM 'UP NORTH', PUT THEM TOGETHER AT AN OPEN AUDITION AND WHAT DO YOU GET?

One of the greatest British pop acts of all time.

From humble beginnings as an unashamedly manufactured boy band, formed in 1990 by manager Nigel Martin-Smith, Take That has emerged as one of the most successful groups in music history. Gary, Mark, Howard, Robbie and Jason have come a long way since the time when they toured schools by day and gay clubs by night – a journey that has been filled with heart-wrenching lows as well as incredible highs.

Now the band has emerged as a stronger, tighter unit than ever. To their huge popularity they can now add credibility, critical acclaim and that most elusive of elements in the music business... longevity. It's a heady mix, but utterly deserved.

So here's to you, boys. Long live Take That.

TAKE...

GARY

NAME:

Gary Barlow

BORN:

20th January 1971

BIRTHPLACE:

Frodsham, Cheshire

STAR SIGN:

Capricorn

SIGNIFICANT OTHERS:

Wife: Dawn
Children: Daniel, Emily and Daisy

INSTRUMENTS:

Piano, keyboards, vocals

EARLY LIFE

The son of agricultural worker
Colin and teacher Marjorie Barlow,
Gary enjoyed a quiet and stable
upbringing with his older brother
Ian. Gary's dad worked hard
to buy his son's first keyboard.
The investment quickly paid off
– in 1986 he reached the semi
finals of the BBC Pebble Mill
songwriting competition with
one of his first compositions,
'Let's Pray For Christmas'.

A TRUE TALENT

Gary is a born songwriter,
having already won five Ivor
Novellos for his work.

WHAT A GUY!

The big-hearted star does huge
amounts of charity work and has
been asked by the Queen to organise
her 85th birthday and Diamond
Jubilee celebrations. In 2009,
Gary organised a charity trek to
the summit of Mount Kilimanjaro
for Children in Need. He is also
planning a charity walk to the
North Pole for BBC Sport Relief.

HOWARD

NAME:

Howard Paul Donald

BORN:

28th April 1968

BIRTHPLACE:

Droylsden, Lancashire

STAR SIGN:

Taurus

SIGNIFICANT OTHERS:

Daughters: Grace and Lola

INSTRUMENTS:

Piano, drums, vocals

EARLY LIFE

One of five siblings, Howard's childhood dream was to be a pilot, despite his showbiz pedigree – mum Kathleen was a singer and dad Keith, an award-winning Latin dance teacher. Unfortunately his parents divorced when he was ten. On leaving school at sixteen, Howard became an apprentice vehicle painter whilst dancing in clubs in his spare time. It was here that he met Jason Orange.

A TRUE TALENT

Howard is a popular house DJ who has performed around the world. He has a huge following in Germany in particular. He is also an accomplished street dancer.

WHAT A GUY!

Howard recently donated 'Unshakeable', a song he wrote but never released, to a little girl called Sophie Dyson. The ten-year-old from Chiswick aims to raise money for the Anthony Nolan charity, helping to save the lives of cancer patients.

TAKE...

JASON

NAME:

Jason Thomas Orange

BORN:

10th July 1970

BIRTHPLACE:

Crumpsall, Manchester

STAR SIGN:

Cancer

SIGNIFICANT OTHERS:

Single, no children

INSTRUMENTS:

Guitar, vocals

EARLY LIFE

Jason grew up with five brothers, including twin Justin and three half-sisters. The clan were raised by his now-divorced parents, Tony and Jenny. After leaving school with no qualifications, Jason worked as a painter and decorator to support himself while honing his dancing skills on the Manchester club scene.

A TRUE TALENT

Jason is an amazing breakdancer whose first TV outing was as a performer on *The Hitman and Her.* In the mid 80s he was a member of prominent breakdance crew 'Street Machine', alongside Howard. The pair began performing as 'Street Beat', going on to place third in the World Breakdancing Championships.

WHAT A GUY!

Jason has played in several charity football matches to raise funds for organisations such as the UK Lowe Syndrome Trust.

MARK

NAME:

Mark Anthony Patrick Owen

BORN:

27th January 1972

BIRTHPLACE:

Oldham, Lancashire

STAR SIGN:

Aquarius

SIGNIFICANT OTHERS:

Wife: Emma
Children: Elwood Jack & Willow Rose

INSTRUMENTS:

Bass guitar, guitar, keyboards,
percussion, vocals

EARLY LIFE

Mark, brother Daniel and sister Tracy
grew up in a small council house with
their father Keith, a decorator, and
mother Mary, a bakery supervisor.
Mark was a proficient footballer with
ambitions to play professionally – he
had trials for Manchester United,
Huddersfield Town and Rochdale
– until an injury ended his dream.
Jobs in a retail boutique and a high
street bank followed. He met Gary
Barlow whilst working as a tea-boy at
Strawberry Studios in Stockport. Not
long after that encounter Mark began
recording backing vocals for him.

A TRUE TALENT

Mark's distinctive vocals have grown and
matured over his career. He plays many
instruments including the Mellotron
keyboard and the koto – a traditional
Japanese stringed instrument.

WHAT A GUY!

In 2010 Mark and the band sang
on 'Everybody Hurts', the REM
cover to raise money for the victims
of the Haiti earthquakes.

ROBBIE

NAME:

Robert Peter Williams

BORN:

13th February 1974

BIRTHPLACE:

Stoke-on-Trent, Staffordshire

STAR SIGN:

Aquarius

SIGNIFICANT OTHERS:

Wife: Ayda Field

INSTRUMENTS:

Guitar, vocals

EARLY LIFE

Robbie Williams was born to publicans Peter and Janet Williams. His father became the licensee at Port Vale FC Social Club, leading to Robbie's lifelong affinity for the team. Always an extrovert, Williams' first taste of the limelight was on stage in school productions – he once played the Artful Dodger in 'Oliver!' Robbie auditioned for Take That straight out of school when his mum spotted an ad in the paper seeking members for a new boy band.

A TRUE TALENT

Robbie has enjoyed a phenomenally successful solo career. He has four entries in the *Guinness Book of Records* including the most Brit awards won by an individual and the most albums to reach UK number one by a male British solo artist.

WHAT A GUY!

Robbie has established a charitable fund called 'Give It Sum' to try to improve local conditions and strengthen community life in North Staffordshire. He also organises Soccer Aid to raise money for UNICEF and works as patron for life-limited children's charity the Donna Louise Trust.

When Take That announced that they were breaking up in February 1996, the chances of the five original members sharing a stage together again seemed slim at best. But during those years apart, Gary, Howard, Mark, Jason and Robbie all felt that something was missing. Despite all the individual success, awards and hit records, it seemed inevitable that the band would finally come home...

The ROAD TO REUNION

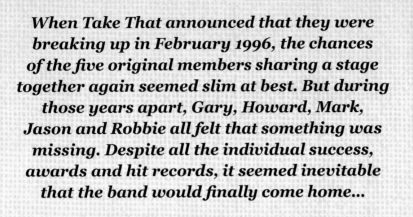

Take That's first rise to fame was glittering and meteoric. In just seven years, the boys were transformed from starry-eyed likely lads to fully-fledged pop icons. The boy band had become one of the biggest acts the UK had ever seen. Success, however, had come at a price. By the mid 90s, the strain was showing. In 1995, Robbie's increasing party lifestyle

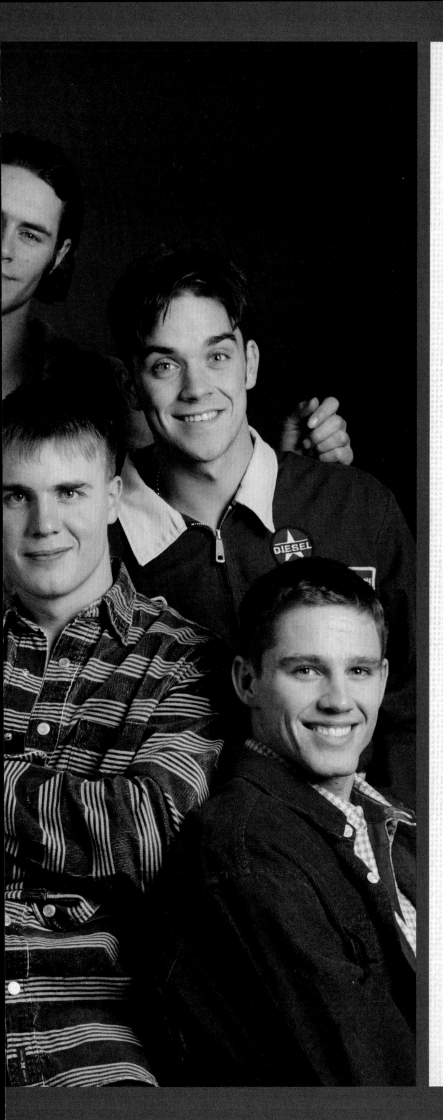

had forced the rest of the band to give him an ultimatum – clean up your act or leave. Robbie left.

Take That continued as a four-piece but, as they all now admit, the thrill had gone. To reach the top, the band had missed out on the carefree teenage years anyone else would take for granted. Whilst their contemporaries were having fun, Gary, Howard, Mark, Jason and Robbie had been living in each other's pockets, working seven-day weeks under intense scrutiny. In short, Take That were burnt out and in need of a change. In February 1996, the remaining members confirmed their split.

As the years passed, a reunion seemed less and less likely. Robbie – the youngest member of the band and the group's unofficial joker – and Gary – Take That's chief songwriter and leader – engaged in a public feud, each blaming each other for the group's demise. To add to the tension, Robbie's solo career went stratospheric, while Gary's faltered.

Meanwhile, Mark seemed content with his life away from the band, releasing several low-key solo records. Howard was carving a niche as a respected DJ and Jason travelled and flirted with an acting career. Getting back together didn't seem to be in any of the boys' minds. The public, however, never gave up hope. The fans still clamoured to see the band together again as they were once were, friends.

After almost ten years apart, the lads were finally brought back together in November 2005 for a TV documentary. *Take That: For The Record* featured interviews with all members of the band, proving a huge hit with viewers. Rumours and whispers of a reunion began to spread like wildfire.

The ROAD TO REUNION

The public didn't have to wait long for the announcement they craved. Just ten days after the documentary aired, the band called a press conference to announce that they were reuniting as a four-piece for a full UK and European tour. Echoing the words when he revealed the band were splitting years earlier, Gary simply told a packed press room, "All the rumours are true, we're getting back together!"

Even after ten years away, Take That were still the hottest ticket in town. The band's 'Ultimate' tour sold out in record time, opening in April 2006 to rave reviews. Now the public wanted more. Gary, Mark, Jason and Howard were quickly offered record deals.

"That first tour was an opportunity to get up there one more time. That seemed like that'd be it. And then we started to get approached about making a record," Mark explained. "There's never been a long term plan. It wasn't like we were back together and it was going to be forever."

Take That were soon back in the studio together, working on new material for the first time in years. The band knew, that if they got it right, they had been given another real chance at success. "I think we came back at the point where our audience were ready to relive their teenage years," says Gary. "The timing was good. And then, the main point, I think we came back with good music. That's usually at the heart of success."

Take That released the album 'Beautiful World' on 9 May 2006, shooting straight to number one. The singles fared just as well. 'Patience' and 'Shine' both hit the top spot and the band started winning important industry awards. Another record-breaking tour followed and a further album, 'Circus'.

Take That were back and bigger than ever, but now the fans were chanting something new. They wanted Robbie.

Turn to page 32 to relive the tears and cheers of Robbie's return...

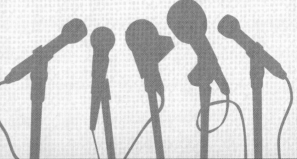

WHO SAID THAT?

It's big news when a band as massive as Take That gets back together after fifteen years apart! Since reuniting in 2010, there's been a lot of talk from each member of the band about the music, tours and their future plans. How closely were you listening? Work your way through these TT sound bites, then write the name of the band member who said each one.

1. 'I think it's a case of we don't need him and he doesn't need us, but why not?'

WHO SAID IT?

2. 'Even though there's never a point where I go, "Right! We're doing this..." It's like I kind of still lead the trail.'

WHO SAID IT?

3. 'I've never been surprised with Take That's success. It's hard to say that without seeming arrogant, but I know that we work hard and there's talent.'

WHO SAID IT?

4. 'I'm meat and two veg, a Mars bar and maybe a cake, all put on the same plate.'

WHO SAID IT?

5. 'I think we could do some great things, not just albums and shows. I always say to the lads we should try and write musicals.'

WHO SAID IT?

6. 'My son loves Rob because he gives him footballs and he gave him a pair of David Beckham's boots the other week.'

WHO SAID IT?

7. 'That's my rebellious side – playing the most underground music possible that no one's ever heard of! And I love it.'

WHO SAID IT?

8. 'I'm not the kind of person who can do nine months [of touring]. I can do two months solid, not a problem. But nine months... I'm not built for it.'

WHO SAID IT?

9. 'One of the two times we met in those ten years was at a charity football match. And he fouled me. Two-footed challenge, could've broken me flipping leg!'

WHO SAID IT?

10. 'In August, we all went to Majorca and caught up for a couple of days. We kind of get the families together now, which is nice to do.'

WHO SAID IT?

11. 'I wouldn't want to happen what we did last time when there was a full stop [at the end of the tour]. Because then it's very difficult to move on. So my ideal would be a comma at the end of the tour.'

WHO SAID IT?

12. 'I've wanted to be in a gang... ever since I wasn't in a gang.'

WHO SAID IT?

13. 'I met this girl and we were getting on really well. She asked me what I did and I just came clean and said, "Actually it's a boy band." It's the first time I've said it with a bit of pride.'

WHO SAID IT?

14. 'It is a great idea to come back after all this time. I just wanted to make sure that the music is absolutely fantastic.'

WHO SAID IT?

15. 'I hated myself in all the pictures in the 1990s, I really did. I'm much happier now than then.'

WHO SAID IT?

IF YOU CAN'T PLACE YOUR VOX POPS,
THE ANSWERS ARE WAITING ON PAGE 93.

THE BANDS
DISCOGRAPHY

ALBUMS

SINGLES

TAKETRIV

Despite being fascinated by cars and motor racing, Robbie has never learned to drive. 'I don't have a driver's licence. In London you just don't drive because the traffic is terrible, so you get cabs everywhere, which has left me being 37 and still without a licence in LA.'

Gary admitted in his autobiography *My Take* that he was on a tube journey from Edgware Road on 7th July 2005 when the train next to him was blown up by a suicide bomber. He says the experience has given him a new perspective on life.

GARY SANG BACKING VOCALS ON ELTON JOHN'S 'CAN YOU FEEL THE LOVE TONIGHT?'

Gary's wife Dawn danced in Timmy Mallet's number one single 'Itsy Bitsy Teeny Weenie Yellow Polka Dot Bikini'. Timmy was also a guest at the couple's tenth wedding anniversary party.

When Gary and Mark started working together they were called 'The Cutest Rush!' After the others joined, the group were going to be 'Kick It'. Finally an interview about Madonna with the headline 'Take That and Party' won the day.

During the last night of the Manchester show in June 2011, Mark and Howard got trapped in the mechanical grip of 20-metre-high robotic man. The huge robot, nicknamed 'Om', broke down during the song 'Love Love'. Robbie giggled, 'Mark, you'll be all right, but Howard you are going to struggle a bit... jump!' The pair were eventually released to the sound of huge cheers.

WHEN HE GETS WRITER'S BLOCK, GARY GOES HOME TO FIND INSPIRATION. 'ONE OF MY BEST TRICKS IS THAT EVERY NOW AND AGAIN, I GO AND SEE MY MUM FOR A FEW DAYS. I LEAVE, AT MY MUM'S HOUSE, A MIDI-KEYBOARD AND A SET OF SPEAKERS. I SET IT UP IN FRONT OF A WINDOW OVERLOOKING A FIELD AND I'M IN A DIFFERENT SITUATION.'

FOR MANY YEARS MARK RECEIVED TWO-THIRDS OF TAKE THAT'S FAN MAIL.

MARK WON THE 2002 SERIES OF CELEBRITY BIG BROTHER, GARNERING A WHOPPING 77% OF THE PUBLIC VOTE.

Before Take That's amazing comeback, short-sighted staff at Madame Tussauds melted down Gary Barlow's wax dummy to make way for a model of Britney Spears.

Robbie once fouled Jason during a charity football match with a dangerous two-footed challenge.

TO ADD TO HIS MANY MUSIC GONGS, GARY HAS WON AWARDS FOR 'REAR OF THE YEAR' (1997) AND 'HAIR OF THE YEAR' (2007).

ROBBIE'S COUSIN'S BROTHER-IN-LAW IS SIMON COWELL.

Howard once owned a tortoise called Winston whilst Mark had an Iguana called Nirvana. He buried it to the sounds of 'Smells Like Teen Spirit'.

JASON STARRED IN THE 1998 LYNDA LA PLANTE SERIES *KILLER NET* ALONGSIDE PAUL BETTANY AND ZOE LUCKER.

The lads were forced for the first time in their career to cancel a show in Copenhagen, Denmark in summer 2011, when Robbie suffered an extreme bout of food poisoning. The poor lad posted a shot of himself laid up, complete with drip to prove to fans just how sick he was.

Jason and Robbie admit they grated on each other in the early days. Jason however was instrumental in breaking the ice and bringing about the reunion. He was the one who phoned Robbie in LA from Manchester after ten years of not speaking.

Since reuniting as a five-piece, Take That have focused everything on the music. Each knockout track is a testimony to how the group have grown and developed as band. Gary, Howard, Mark, Robbie and Jason have all poured their hearts and souls into the lyrics, setting each new melody alight with their poignant phrases and meaningful rhymes.

Take That tunes are poetry in motion, but how well do you know each line? Study each of the lyrics, then write in the songs they come from. The cloud of songs titles on the facing page should help you get started.

LET'S GET LYRICAL

What Do You Want From Me?

Wait

Underground Machine

Eight Letters

Aliens

Love Love Kidz SOS The Flood

Affirmation Wonderful World Man

Happy Now Pretty Things

When We Were Young

1. *'The monkeys learned to build machines, they think they'll get to heaven through the universe.'*

2. *'Watch your mouth son, or you'll find yourself floating home.'*

3. *'You're much too strong for me, and I can't hold your hand like I used to.'*

4. *'It's getting harder, harder to recover from the night before.'*

5. *'Is it a question of force? A metaphysical law?'*

6. *'Under mind control, we'll be practicing our politics, defending our policies, preparing for apocalypse.'*

7. *'And every day was how we dreamed, never knowing the cost of what we paid letting someone else be strong.'*

8. *'I'm a supersonic specimen, a minor miracle of medicine.'*

9. *'We'll take you right back down to Earth from the Motherland, this is a first class journey from the Gods to the Son of Man.'*

10. *'All the counterfeited scream tonight, when the elevated become illuminated.'*

11. *'Youth don't leave me, hair stay on me. God, I love those hips.'*

12. *'In this moment where we exist, on the precipice of the abyss, it always was how it is.'*

13. *'You might be good looking, but you can't sleep with yourself tonight.'*

14. *'We became the parade on the streets that we once cleaned, expendable soldiers smiling at anything.'*

15. *'Oh no! I've fallen off a pedestal, and your selected memory is really quite incredible.'*

Take That were at the top of their game all over again, but the band still felt incomplete. Gary, Mark, Howard and Jason all sensed it. It was time for Robbie to turn Take That back into a five-piece...

REUNTITED

While his old bandmates were enjoying their second lease of fame, Robbie's solo career was changing. His most recent album, 'Rudebox', had received a mixed reaction from fans and critics alike, and, now based in Los Angeles, Robbie's enthusiasm was waning. "The edge was gone, because that's not where your heart is any more," Robbie said later. "Half of the last record was electronic and half was kind of old Robbie and I didn't really want to do old Robbie."

But it was in Los Angeles, Robbie's adopted hometown, where the seeds for a full reunion were sown. The band reached out to their missing member, and after a few false starts, the five got together again for a meeting in a hotel room.

"At some point, as the song goes, I'd thrown everybody underneath the bus, so I didn't know how they were going to greet me, whether they were going to greet me at all," Robbie revealed. "It was great and bad. Great because there was obviously a really good vibe going on between the boys themselves – and great because I could feel part of it. But bad because I'd got words with Gary that I needed to be spoken."

Needing a chance to clear the air, Robbie and Gary agreed to meet again. "The following night we had the: 'You said I was fat in 1991' talk," Gary explained. "We got to the end of it and we all said it would be good to do something, like a one-off single. And sure enough, we didn't hear from Rob for four or five months!"

The following summer, Gary holidayed in Los Angeles again and once more got in touch with Robbie. The pair decided to write some new music together. Over two nights the pair wrote a clutch of new material. The bridges had been rebuilt and Gary and Robbie had proved they could work together again – only one question remained.

"I sat down and said to Robbie, I'm going home next week – what is this? What are we doing here?" Gary admitted. "And he said, that's it now, we've done it – I want to work with the lads!"

And with that, the once seemingly impossible had happened. Take That were back!

AND THE
Award
GOES TO…

Take That's accolades are varied and many – from Brit awards to praise for the eye-popping theatre of their live shows. Go back through the years and relive some of TT's major triumphs…

2011 Phonographic Performance Limited Award, Most Played UK Artist

Spex German Entertainment Award Best Music Video ('Kidz')

Greatest Event Ever at Wembley Stadium ('Circus Live Tour')

ECHO Award, Best International Group

BRIT Award, Best British Group

Virgin Media Award, Best Group

2010 Q Award, Hall of Fame

2009 GQ Men of the Year Award, Best Band

Q Award, Best Live Act

Q Award, Best Single ('Greatest Day')

Nordoff Robbins Silver Clef Award, Outstanding Contribution to UK music

2008 Ivor Novello Award, Most Performed Work ('Shine')

Virgin Media Award, Best Single ('Rule The World')

Sony Ericsson Tour of the Year Award, ('Take That Arena Tour')

BRIT Award, Best British Single ('Shine')

Brit Award, Best British Live Act

2007 BRIT Award, Best British Single ('Patience')

2006 Q Idol Award

1996 BRIT Award, Best British Single ('Back For Good')

1995 MTV Europe Music Awards, Best Live Act

Nordoff Robbins Music Awards, Silver Clef, Outstanding Contribution to UK Music

1994 BRIT Award, Best British Single ('Pray')

BRIT Award, Best British Video ('Pray')

MTV Europe Music Award, Best Group

1993 BRIT Award, Best British Single ('Could It Be Magic')

PROGRESS

HOW DID TAKE THAT COME UP WITH HITS LIKE 'THE FLOOD' AND 'LOVE LOVE'? TAKE A PEEK BEHIND-THE-SCENES TO SEE HOW THE BAND PUT TOGETHER THEIR RECORD-BREAKING COMEBACK ALBUM...

Look inside the sleeve of the album 'Progress', and its follow-up EP, 'Progressed', and you'll notice something different from all previous Take That albums. For the first time, under the credits section it reads, 'All songs written and composed by Jason Orange, Gary Barlow, Howard Donald, Mark Owen and Robbie Williams.'

'IT WAS JUST THE FIVE OF US IN A ROOM MAKING THIS ALBUM, NO ONE ELSE. IT HAD TO BE THAT WAY.' GARY

Although, written and recorded nearly a year later, work on the album really began when the band first reconnected with Robbie in Los Angeles. After clearing

the air between them, Gary and Robbie understood that if they were going to reform as a five-piece, they had to be able to write material together.

'IN THE PAST, WE HAD TO LIE A LOT IN THIS BAND. NOW WE, WE JUST WANTED TO TELL THE TRUTH.' ROBBIE

Robbie and Gary worked quickly and easily together and were proud of the results. "That writing session was quite amazing I thought," Gary excitedly remembered. "Even though we were singing into a small mic, the way he was singing was great – someone who was really good at what they did. I was respecting him and he was respecting me. All the time I was thinking I'd got to get him in with the lads, because if it went as well we were going to be rocking! It all came together with the band after that."

Once the full band finally got together to write the record, they needed to agree how the album was going to sound. Gary had already prepared a selection of demos to show the boys what he had in mind. "To actually sit in for the first time and Gary bring you a load of backing tracks. To hear that stuff is like, what the heck have you been listening to?! Then he tells you about the history of electronic pop music in England. And you're like, 'Oh. You know that too... brilliant.' And we were away." The band were all on the same page.

After settling on a more electronic sound, the boys picked producer Stuart Price to help them turn their ideas into a reality. Price is a veteran of the UK electronic scene, earning himself an impressive reputation when he produced Madonna's album, 'Hard Candy', and her subsequent live tour. With everything and everyone in place, Take That were ready.

While excited to get started, there was one member who felt nervous about the writing and recording that lay ahead. "My biggest insecurity had always been, what do I contribute to the band?" Jason confessed. "I don't really write music or understand it like the others do. I was chosen back in the day for my dancing skills." But once the sessions began, Jason's confidence began to grow. Soon he was playing a key role in the writing process.

While Gary had been preparing musical ideas, Robbie admitted he spent the months before the sessions collecting lyrics. "Being in a band again, you've got four other people with you that you can't let down and that you really want to impress," Robbie explained. "I wanted to go in there fully armed."

Once together, Mark, Jason and Howard added their input. The guys brainstormed melodies, suggested lyrical ideas and helped to decide how the songs should be put together. With the newfound spirit of openness in the band they worked quickly. For the first time Take That had produced an album that all the members could truly enjoy and be proud of.

The results are there for us all to share. It doesn't take a music industry expert to tell that from the resulting record and tour ticket sales, we all enjoyed it too!

PROGRESS

Released 15th November 2010

1. The Flood
2. SOS
3. Wait
4. Kidz
5. Pretty Things
6. Happy Now
7. Underground Machine
8. What Do You Want From Me?
9. Affirmation
10. Eight Letters/Flowerbed (Hidden Track)

PROGRESSED

Released 13th June 2011

[2 disk extended album]

1. When We Were Young
2. Man
3. Love Love
4. The Day The Work Is Done
5. Beautiful
6. Don't Say Goodbye
7. Aliens
8. Wonderful World

FROM **BOY BAND** TO GROWN-UP GROUP

Their 'Progress' album cover may picture the lads evolving from apes to men, but their evolution in terms of attitude, style and sound is nothing short of astonishing. No pop group can have matured more in the last two decades.

STYLE

When the boys first got together, their style could be summed up as 'less is less'. Early photoshoots saw them posing for the camera clad in novelty boxer shorts and boxing gloves, western style chaps, even completely naked save for their boots! Thankfully their look quickly progressed to include items of clothing – although from the sporty US jock theme to the all-leather look – it took a while for them to find their style.

These days the lads have given their wardrobe a much needed overhaul, becoming style icons for men in their thirties and forties. Award ceremonies and formal soirées see them suited, booted and perfectly coordinated, whilst expressing each of their distinct styles. Gary and Jason love smart tailoring and crew necks. Howard gives an urban twist to his look by pairing beanies and tees with smart jackets. Mark's indie style involves pork pie hats and rakish neck ties. Fashion-forward Robbie loves vests, military jackets and the latest sports wear.

HAIR

It's good to know that even the rich and famous weren't always so groomed! The boys had bad hair days a-plenty before finding what worked for them. Remember Gary's spiky peroxide crop? Jason's shaved head with goatee and train tracks? How about Howard's grungy dreads and Robbie and Mark's mop-tops and curtains? Thankfully, good sense and good hairdressers have since prevailed – the lads currently boast dos to be proud of.

STAGE

Early shows were all about the synchronised dance routines – staging was basic to say the least. In their first gigs, the boys were lucky to get a stool to perch on for the ballads! Over the years the staging and production of TT's outings have become ever more elaborate. The concerts have graduated from the pyrotechnics of the 'Relight My Fire' days to sophisticated robots, incredible acrobatics and polished, hard-hitting dance routines. All of this makes a Take That event an awesome spectacle to behold.

ATTITUDE

At first Gary, Mark, Howard, Donald and Robbie were not slow to avail themselves of the perks of fame. These days it's early nights all round during the gruelling tour schedule, with professionalism being the key. As for the dynamics between group members – the fireworks just aren't there any more. Old rivalries have been consigned to history. The band recently rubbished claims that they've have fallen out with Robbie again. During the making of 'Progress', Robbie summed it up as, "we don't need each other any more, we want each other."

SOUND

Take That's sound has matured, while remaining accessible and true. Now their lyrics are emotive and often based on personal experience. 'Shame' is based on Gary and Robbie's feud, and 'Nobody Else' is dedicated to Gary's parents. Songwriting in Take That was once the responsibility of Gary alone. But, since their reunion, all the band members have had a hand in creating new material.

This time around, all the band members' voices are heard, too. Mark sings lead on 'Shine' and 'Kidz'. Howard first sang lead on 'Never Forget', but in recent years has taken the mic for 'Beautiful World', 'What Is Love', 'Here' and 'Mancunian Way'. Even Jason performs solo, lending his talents to 'How Did It Come To This' and 'Flowerbed'.

TAKE THAT

TAKE A LOOK AT TAKE THAT'S INCREDIBLE VITAL STATISTICS - THE NUMBERS NEVER LIE!

1 Solo single recorded, but never released, by Howard.

3 Number of solo Mark Owen records.

5 Ivor Novello Awards won by Gary Barlow.

8 The number of siblings Jason Orange has.

10 '...legged national treasure' - the phrase used to describe the band in a BBC album review.

16 Robbie's age when he joined Take That.

16 The number of top five hits Gary has written.

17 Robbie's record-breaking haul of Brit Awards.

18 Take That songs featuring Mark on lead vocals.

20 Om's (the 'Progress' tour's robot) height in metres.

77 Percentage of the public vote Mark received when he won Celebrity Big Brother.

135 Recording-breaking number of weeks that Robbie has appeared in the German top ten.

54,000 Members of the audience at the band's comeback show in Sunderland.

BY NUMBERS

300,000
Downloads of the Take That 'Progress' app.

432,490
Copies of the album 'The Circus' sold in its first week on sale in the UK – the third highest figure ever.

520,000
The number of copies the full reunion album 'Progress' sold in its first week – the second highest total ever.

1.8 million
People who saw the reunited band live on their 'Progress' tour.

40 million
Records sold by Take That during the course of their career.

In His Own Words:
GARY

Gary on...

missing Rob...
"I spent fifteen years thinking about what I was going to say."

pre-reunion jitters...
"We were just really excited to see him."

that chat...
"All these things had been built up for so long it just sounded stupid as it was coming out. We just needed to sit opposite each other and talk."

hitting the big 40...
"People still find it hard to believe I'm forty. Actually I'm not bothered about age. I'm really happy and it's lovely to be forty, I'd recommend it to anyone. Music is a young person's industry, but you want a few of the older bands like us around."

fame...
"It was our whole life last time – we didn't have time for anything else. But we do have other lives now - it's only half our life. We're in control now and it's nice to be in control of your own destiny."

karma...
"Our manager taught us the first time round to always be nice to everyone. I feel like we got to the end of the reign in the '90s and we had been nice to everyone. It's unbelievable now how many of those people are now the heads of Radio 1 and the president of Sony Records. And everyone we've bumped into has been glad to see us."

> "I SPENT FIFTEEN YEARS THINKING ABOUT WHAT I WAS GOING TO SAY."

becoming a father...
"On 16th August, 2000, our son Daniel was born. Talk about putting a new perspective on things. Dan was, after Dawn, the best thing that had ever happened to me."

working together again...
"We are really enjoying each other at the moment and I do feel like our work in the studio is actually just beginning. We have got off to a great start and we are enjoying working with each other so much, we do it over the Internet, we do it whenever we can."

ironing out the kinks...
"Part of us coming back as a five was to right the wrongs. We felt we should have looked after Rob better the first time round, we're looking after him this time."

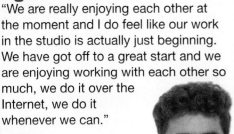

GARY

As well as being the driving force behind the sound of Take That, Gary Barlow spends his time outside the band working on a long and diverse list of musical projects. His first love has always been songwriting – over the years he has penned hits for many artists including Delta Goodrem, Blue, Charlotte Church, Donny Osmond and Will Young. The star's phenomenal talent was confirmed in 2009 when a poll voted him the Greatest British Songwriter Ever! Even Beatles greats Paul McCartney and John Lennon couldn't knock our boy off the top spot.

But when the awards, trophies and plaudits are locked away in their display cases, what is the real Gary Barlow like? Even though he's a self-confessed workaholic, the singer is also a devoted family man. He has been happily married to his wife Dawn for many years and is dad to three gorgeous children. Gary first met Dawn when she cast as a dancer on Take That's 1995 'Nobody Else' tour. The pair have been each other's rocks ever since. With Gary Barlow, what you see is what you get – a genuinely nice guy, who remembers his roots and gives thanks every day.

THERE'S ONLY ONE GARY BARLOW BECAUSE...

- ...despite his crazy schedule, he continues to work tirelessly for charity. Gary and Dawn even managed to raise funds for Barnado's during their tenth wedding anniversary bash!

- ...his honest approach and musical insight have landed him the plumjob of Simon Cowell's replacement on The X Factor.

- ...he's managed to earn himself a Blue Peter gold badge for outstanding achievements and services to children.

- ...Her Majesty the Queen has asked Gary to plan her 85th birthday and Diamond Jubilee celebrations.

- ...he's the modest boy next door with a heart of solid gold – the ultimate national treasure!

DESPITE HIS CRAZY SCHEDULE, HE CONTINUES TO WORK TIRELESSLY FOR CHARITY.

GARY'S PHENOMENAL TALENT
WAS CONFIRMED IN 2009
WHEN A POLL VOTED HIM
THE GREATEST BRITISH
SONGWRITER EVER!

Thomas Sabo

german

53

UPCLOSE
&PERSONAL

A whole generation has grown up with the boys in their lives – through good times and bad, triumphs and trials. Now it's time to probe a little deeper. This quiz will test how well you really know Robbie, Gary, Mark, Howard and Jason. Reach for your biro and pull on your Take That thinking caps...

QUESTION 1

Aside from being a well-respected DJ and dance music producer, Howard also plays two traditional instruments. What are they?

QUESTION 2

Jason's first big opportunity came when he was asked to appear on the 1980s show, The Hitman And Her. What was it that Jason could do that caught the eye of the show's producers?

QUESTION 3

Mark Owen has two middle names. Patrick is one, can you name the other?

QUESTION 4

Being the main songwriter for the band, Gary has won a host of trophies including several prestigious Ivor Novello Awards. Exactly how many Ivors has Gary bagged to date?

QUESTION 5

Robbie Williams is arguably Port Vale Football Club's most famous supporter. What prompted him to start supporting the club?

QUESTION 6

After the band broke up, Jason briefly forged a career as an actor. Despite appearing on television and on stage, why did he ultimately give up?

QUESTION 7

To date, Mark Owen is the only member of the band to appear in a reality TV show. He won the 2002 celebrity version of a popular show by a landslide margin in the final public vote. What was the show?

QUESTION 8

In his time away from the band, Howard recorded a solo single that was never released. What was it called?

QUESTION 9

Gary's a self-confessed music workaholic. In addition to his time with the band, writing for other artists and running his own management company, he also appears as the head judge on which UK talent show?

QUESTION 10

To the nearest five million, how many records has Robbie sold as a solo artist?

QUESTION 11

Which of the following artists has Gary not written material for – Will Young, N-Dubz or Nicola Roberts?

QUESTION 12

Robbie shares the lead vocals with Gary on four tracks on the album 'Progress'. How many songs feature their twin lead vocals on the follow-up release, 'Progressed'?

QUESTION 13

Shortly before the band reformed, Jason achieved four A-levels from South Trafford College. Can you name one of the four subjects he studied?

QUESTION 14

Mark regularly shares lead vocal duties, but only sings the solo lead on one song from the album 'Progress'. What is it called?

QUESTION 15

The band released 'Kidz' as the second single from the album 'Progress'. Howard produced a dance remix of the track for the release. What was it called?

UP CLOSE & PERSONAL

JASON

"AFTER A YEAR OF LIVING AND BREATHING TOGETHER WE'RE STARTING TO PROGRESS…"

Jason on…

being a success…

"Being a good pop band is not just about good pop songs. It's about a good story. Our story is pretty good."

breaking the ice with Robbie…

"I hadn't spoken to him for ten years. Maybe once or twice in passing, but not a deep conversation. But we spoke for hours on the phone. He helped me make the decision to go back with the lads."

Take That's return to the top…

"There's not a night on stage when there's not a moment when we look at each other and it's like, 'what are we still doing here?'"

the reunion…

"I'm over the moon that Robbie's back with us, however long it lasts. I just want to enjoy our time with him. Life is beautifully strange sometimes."

getting to know each other again…

"After a year of living and breathing together we're starting to progress… starting our journey together."

the buzz of performing…

"When we've come to the show and at the end [of the show] there's absolute delight on people's faces. Seeing that en masse is when it hits you. It's brilliant."

fashion…

"I'm not as into shopping as the other lads… I'm a northern lad – all I need is a good jacket and I'm happy."

travelling…

"I spent quite a lot of the ten years we had off travelling round Europe and Asia, then come back and go to America, come back and go to Australia. A month here, a month there. The longest I was away in one swoop was a year, that was Asia and part of North America. I loved it, the old backpack and all that."

love…

"I still feel too young to get married. I would really want to and I would love to have kids. At the moment, I like life the way it is…"

"BEING A GOOD POP BAND IS NOT JUST ABOUT GOOD POP SONGS. IT'S ABOUT A GOOD STORY. OUR STORY IS PRETTY GOOD."

JASON

Jason Orange is a something of an enigma – a private man who is happy to stay in the background during the rounds of press junkets and interviews that is part and parcel of being in Take That. Everything changes however, the instant he steps on stage. Jason's mesmerising dance presence, energy and sheer physicality combine to entrance the audience time and time again. In recent years, Jason has started to play the guitar during live gigs, too.

Away from the celebrity circuit, Jason is older, wiser and happier than ever before. Whilst Gary, Howard and Mark are all fathers, he remains a committed singleton. Living without ties has given the star a unique freedom. During the years that the band were apart he travelled all over the world, meeting people and experiencing new things. Jason doesn't rule out marriage and babies, but for the time being at least, he is more than content seeing where the Take That rollercoaster will lead him next.

THERE'S ONLY ONE JASON ORANGE BECAUSE...

- ...in between Take That's reign at the top of the charts, he had the determination to go back and put himself through South Trafford college – earning A-Levels in psychology, biology, history and sociology.

- ...he stepped forward in 2007 to sing lead vocals in 'Wooden Boat' – the first time he'd ever taken the mic and carried a Take That song.

- ...he pulled off an unforgettable old-school breakdancing battle with Howard in every performance of the Progress live tour. He sure knows how to throw some moves!

- ...he takes time to give back to the fans – signing autographs, chatting and posing for photos.

- ...he's a traditional Northern boy with an irresistible smile and a cheeky sense of humour.

HE'S A TRADITIONAL NORTHERN BOY WITH AN IRRESISTIBLE SMILE AND A CHEEKY SENSE OF HUMOUR.

AWAY FROM THE CELEBRITY
CIRCUIT, JASON IS OLDER,
WISER AND HAPPIER
THAN EVER BEFORE.

Children In Need...

In 2009, Gary Barlow organised one of the most amazing concerts in the history of British pop. Children In Need Rocks was a musical spectacular staged in the hallowed setting of the Royal Albert Hall. In addition to an exclusive set from Gary, Howard, Mark and Jason; a glittering array of stars queued-up to lend their talents to the show. Sir Paul McCartney, Dizzee Rascal, Dame Shirley Bassey, Lily Allen and many more joined in to perform and raise money for the charity. Between them, the all-star cast could boast an impressive hoard of over fifty number-one singles!

"I've always wanted to do something like this and I can promise a night to remember, a night that will, I hope, play a small part in changing the lives of disadvantaged children across the UK." - *Gary*.

The event was a dazzling success, generating a staggering £2,000,000 for Children In Need. The 4,500-strong audience and millions watching at home were treated to Cheryl Cole duetting with Snow Patrol, a knockout performance by Leona Lewis and Paul McCartney leading a rousing finale of 'Hey Jude'.

It had all the ingredients of a musical fairytale, but Gary had one extra surprise up his sleeve. When Take That finished their set, they welcomed someone very special on stage... Robbie.

The Albert Hall erupted as the boys hugged and waved. For the first time

ROCKS!!!

in years Robbie and the lads were together again! It was a night none of the guys will ever forget. Although they were still some months away from a full reunion, they'd made their first public step. It was official – Take That and Robbie were talking again.

'I was tearing up when I was on stage with the lads. I love them – there's no more hard feelings.' - *Robbie*.

nearly blocked by an unlikely public figure – Prime Minister David Cameron! On the night of the show, the PM visited Take That's dressing room to offer some words of encouragement. While Gary and the boys were chatting, Mr Cameron became aware that someone was trying to get into the room. He carried on regardless, worried that an interruption would end his chance to chat with the band. It was only when the Prime Minister decided to leave that Robbie was discovered waiting in the corridor outside! Luckily Rob

was philosophical about the whole experience, saying "We've only been waiting fourteen years for a reunion – five more minutes won't hurt!'

Since that amazing night, the boys have each gone on to lead many more inspiring charity initiatives. In September 2010, Robbie headlined at a huge concert for Help For Heroes, performing for over 60,000 at the Twickenham Stadium. Delighted fans were even treated to an exclusive live duet, as Gary and Robbie sang 'Shame'.

JOIN THE
CHORUS
LINE

Ask Gary and he'll tell you, 'Pop songs are all about the choruses'. In their time, Take That have written some of the most famous bridges ever. Sing along to some of their best anthems, then fill in the missing words.

1. 'And when I went away, what I forgot to say, was all I had to say,

three words, one meaning.'

2. 'There'll be trouble when the kidz come out, there'll be lots for them to

'

3. 'What a wonderful world this is, what a

of bliss.'

4. 'Although no one understood, we were holding back the flood, learning how to

.'

5. 'And why don't you teach your

and give you love love.'

6. 'Ain't got the strength to fight anymore, got no desire to

I need an affirmation.'

7. So collectible, why not collect them all?

, all those pretty things, God bless those pretty things.'

8. 'When we were young, we

.'

9. 'I feel myself falling, I'm feeling

.'

10. 'What do you want from me? I, I still

,

,

11. Don't say goodbye to the world, until

'

.'

12. 'It's an SOS, an SOS, like a

it's an SOS.'

13. 'Wait, there's something I

,

something I hid away.'

14. 'When the work is done, the work is done , we'll be

the circuits of our minds.'

15. 'Man, complicated,

,

,

fragile man.'

The Videos

Imaginative videos have always been an integral part of each new Take That single release. Each one is a capsule movie made with care, exacting standards and astonishing creativity. What will the band surprise us with next? The theme is bound to be unexpected, but one element can be guaranteed – the next video is sure to be set against the most awesome soundtrack ever!

The Flood

According to director Mat Whitecross, the lads came up with the concept for this stunning video themselves. For their first track as a reformed unit they wanted an epic feel, describing it as 'Chariots of Fire meets Forrest Gump'.

The final Flood storyline saw the boys taking part in a rowing race up the Thames. The band ultimately loses the race, but once past the finish line they each row off towards the horizon and open water. The National Rowing Coach for Team GB agreed to train the boys for the shoot, but originally said they'd need three months to get them to a basic proficiency level.

Unfortunately TT's packed schedule meant they had only one night free for a crash-course in boating!

Five-seater sculling boats were custom-made for the band along with old-fashioned white kits complete with a bespoke Take That crest. The majority of the shoot was shot on Dorney Lake, near Eton in Buckinghamshire, soon to be the location of the London 2012 Olympic rowing events. Special permission had to be obtained so that the latter part of the story could be filmed outside the Houses of Parliament. This was shot at the

crack of dawn, with the lads being tailed by a low-flying helicopter and flanked by safety boats.

The polished end product actually belies the troubled and complex filming process. One of the boys capsized during training and then the final part of the video had to be abandoned after the boat hit a rock and sank! Whitecross later admitted, "If we'd known how difficult it would be to shoot on water, I think we'd have ended up doing the whole thing in the studio."

Kidz

Whitecross decided to team up with Eran Creevy for the next Take That release. The video was shot during two chilly February days on location in Bulgaria. 'Kidz' was another big production – the sequence featured a CGI spaceship, SWAT teams, the army, a host of Humvees, ambulances and armoured vehicles, a fake helicopter and 200 police extras!

The 'Kidz' storyboard showed a world consumed by rioting and warfare being shocked into peace. The cause? An otherworldly visit from Take That, descending to Earth in their spaceship to bring unity through music. Afterwards

Creevy said, "It was great working with Take That, they have great visual ideas and like to have an open dialogue with the director."

So is the video, as some have suggested, really a social commentary on the current political climate in the Middle East? Creevy laughs at the idea, explaining that. "We just wanted Take That to fly a spaceship in the shape of their logo and get the chance to create a Hollywood aesthetic."

Turn to page 88 to reveal more behind-the-scenes secrets from Take That's most famous videos.

HOWARD

Howard on...

reforming as a four-piece...

"When you get the four of us together, there's a real magic, something people respond to. They see the friendship and the commitment. Good songs, hard graft and chemistry – that's Take That."

working with Robbie first time around...

"I kind of realise now how young he was and what happened, and you don't really know what's going through his head. I didn't really... I did care, but it just happened so fast and... I wish I'd said something."

playing his part in 'Progress'...

"I haven't got the confidence. I need someone to give me a kick up the arse to come forward. That's exactly what I did with this album – I came up with backing tracks, and me and Gary would work on them together. Out of the ten we might have done, we ended up using three of them."

the end results...

"I feel really proud. It's really energetic and fresh. I've been so much more involved in this album than any other."

being a DJ...

"I was DJ-ing before the group started. I got my first set of turntables in 1987 out of a catalogue. I was doing mixes of old-school hip-hop."

wowing the dance floor...

"When you're DJ-ing you really don't know what's going to happen next. You've got an idea, but most of the time you're watching the dance floor, trying to determine where to take the music. For me, that just adds to the excitement."

the here and now...

"This is about life. This is about the five of us."

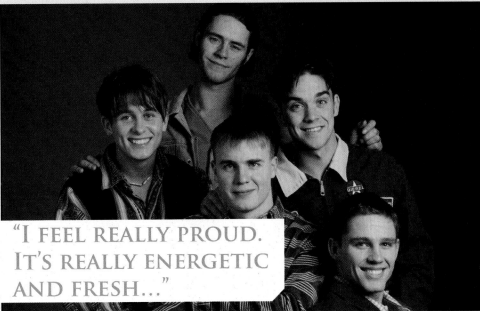

> "I FEEL REALLY PROUD. IT'S REALLY ENERGETIC AND FRESH..."

meeting Robbie again...

"He was just the same person that I'd remembered in the group, really warm-hearted. Whether he felt embarrassed or outnumbered I don't know, but it really clicked. We met again in LA and it was all really nice, and that's where it started."

the reunion...

"I think it's a case of we don't need him and he doesn't need us, but why not?"

> "THIS IS ABOUT LIFE. THIS IS ABOUT THE FIVE OF US."

HOWARD

As well as being a formidable breakdancer and a respected house DJ, Howard Donald has a special role within the band. The group's vocal sound is largely down to the shy Mancunian – a rich backing harmony that puts the distinctive Take That stamp onto every new hit record. Howard's quiet modesty make it easy to overlook this secret ingredient, but all his band mates will tell you how important it is.

As a DJ, Howard has toured the world many times over, stopping everywhere from Ibiza to Lithuania. Combine that level of travel with Take That's commitments and you notch up a lot of airmails! Howard has another reason for being a frequent flyer – his two daughters live in two different countries. The star adores his girls Grace and Lola, always making sure he's there to share the important stuff in each of their lives.

THERE'S ONLY ONE HOWARD DONALD BECAUSE…

- …he gives knockout live DJs sets under his name DJ HD. His club following in Germany is especially huge.

- …despite suffering a collapsed lung after throwing a backflip on the 'Beautiful World' tour, he managed to recover himself quickly enough to return for the final leg.

- …his interests spread far and wide. In June 2011, Howard invested in a brand new American seaplane, with the eventual goal of earning his pilot's licence.

- …he sings the poignant lead vocals on 'Never Forget'.

- …he has an easygoing manner, gentle enthusiasm and a quiet role as peacemaker within the band.

…HE GIVES KNOCKOUT LIVE DJs SETS UNDER HIS NAME DJ HD. HIS CLUB FOLLOWING IN GERMANY IS ESPECIALLY HUGE.

Let's Get Together

When you're in one of the biggest bands the UK has ever seen, you get your pick of the best artists to work with. Over the years, the boys have collaborated with pop icons, legendary divas and rising hip hop stars. Here's a celebration of some of the best.

Artist: *Lulu*
Song: *'Relight My Fire'*
Probably Take That's most famous collaboration was recorded in 1993 with 60s star Lulu. The infectious hit was a cover of a 1979 disco track by Dan Hartman. 'Relight My Fire' went straight in at number one and became a staple of the band's live set. It gave Lulu her first chart-topper and another musical first. Coming twenty-nine years after her debut single, it was officially the longest time it has ever taken an artist to reach the top spot.

Artist: *Beverley Knight*
Song: *'Relight My Fire' Live*
Soul star Beverley was picked to be the lead support act for the band on their Circus tour. She also joined them onstage every night to handle Lulu's vocals in Relight My Fire. They've remained friends since and recently Beverley, who's opposed to TV talent shows, has been asking Gary to use his influence to change The X Factor's format.

> *"They are divas and really high maintenance! They stay to the bitter end at a party, too. And they do disagree on things. If everyone is saying A is the right answer then Jason Orange will say it's B."* - **Beverley**

Artist: *Fake That*
Song: *'Happy Now'*

For 2011's Comic Relief appeal, Take That made a special video with tribute act Fake That. Not heard of Fake That? You'll probably be familiar with their members. Comedians Kevin Bishop, Catherine Tate, David Walliams, James Cordon and Alan Carr each played a band member in the hilarious video.

> *"Being in a boy band for the day was really tiring. We had to do all the dance moves – but when Take That did them they were like twenty-two – I'm thirty-nine, and I just thought 'I can't handle this!'"* **- David Walliams**

Artist: *Kylie Minogue*
Song: *'Kids'*

Robbie and Kylie were at the peak of their fame when they recorded this cheeky track in 2000. Robbie was in the studio recording his solo album, 'Sing When You're Winning', when he received a call from Kylie asking if he'd write a song for her. Robbie jumped at the chance, but after writing the song, he realised he like it too much to give it away. Solution? To propose it as a duet instead.

> *"I've always had a crush on Kylie, ever since she wore dungarees in Neighbours. I saw the lyrics as an excuse to make her sing lots of dirty words, but I chickened out!"* **- Robbie**

Artist: *N-Dubz*
Song: *'No One Knows'*

As well as being Take That's main writer and a father of three, Gary continues to write and produce music for other artists. In 2009, he surprised everyone by appearing on a track with urban trio N-Dubz for their album 'Against All Odds'. Gary and N-Dubz vocalist Tulisa have recently found themselves working together again, this time on The X Factor judging panel.

> *"He came in the studio and it was great – he had time for the underdogs and he came and wrote a smashing hook. We've done a big tune with Gary Barlow. We're not narrow-minded you get me, we can make big tunes, and we can make massive hooks, big concepts that's why we've got Gary Barlow in. It ain't Take That, it's Take Braaaap. Legend..."* **- Fazer, N-Dubz**

Artist: *Lily Allen*
Song: *'Who'd Have Known?/Shine'*

After listening to the recordings of her own song, 'Who'd Have Known?' Lily Allen knew that she'd never be able to release it herself – the tune was too similar to one of her favourite Take That songs, 'Shine'. Instead, Lily came clean about her inspiration and posted it online. It instantly became a fan favourite. Lily went on to perform the song at the 2010 Children In Need concert, joined onstage by four special guests to mash the track up with 'Shine'.

Artist: *Pet Shop Boys*
Song: *'No Regrets' and 'Progress' tour*

All the boys admit to being huge fans of the Pet Shop Boys, so the duo were an obvious choice when picking a lead support band for their comeback tour. Robbie had worked with them previously on the track 'No Regrets' from his second solo album, 'I've Been Expecting You.' Written about his split from the band, there was press speculation about whether he would perform it on the Progress tour, but it's actually one of the songs the band use to close their set.

> *"Pet Shop Boys was the first CD I ever bought. I've followed their whole career and always loved their unique approach to records and live performance. That combined with two lovely people means we're in for a great time."* **- Gary**

MARK

Mark on...

growing up...
"We knew how to be pop stars before we knew how to be men."

the chances of reunion...
"We managed to get ourselves to a place where the bridge was easier to walk over."

being five again...
"We make the effort to talk. I think we can turn to each other now. We've got more in common and I think there's a lot more soul in us now."

making music with Rob...
"Getting the five of us in a room together, although always a dream, never actually seemed like becoming a reality. Now the reality of the five of us making a record together feels like a dream. It's been an absolute delight spending time with Rob again. But I'm still a better footballer."

taking it slow...
"The whole process of being back together . . . almost in the back of your mind you're not sure that you really are together. Do you know what I mean? There's never been a long-term plan . . . It wasn't like we were back together and it was going to be forever. I think we've done everything by baby steps."

how things have changed...
"It's been an amazing journey. There's a new honesty. We don't have to pretend any more."

'Do You Want From Me...'
"My hope for me and my relationship, and with Emma, is in that song. You know I want us to grow old together."

hanging out together...
"In August we all went to Majorca and caught up for a couple of days. We get the families together, which is nice to do. That's something for me... beyond the music, there's a relationship between us all."

the craziness of living in the Big Brother house...
"I had a moment where I woke up, and at one end of the room Les Dennis was shaving, and at the other end Goldie was putting on his aftershave. I thought – what am I doing here?"

"WE KNEW HOW TO BE POP STARS BEFORE WE KNEW HOW TO BE MEN."

MARK

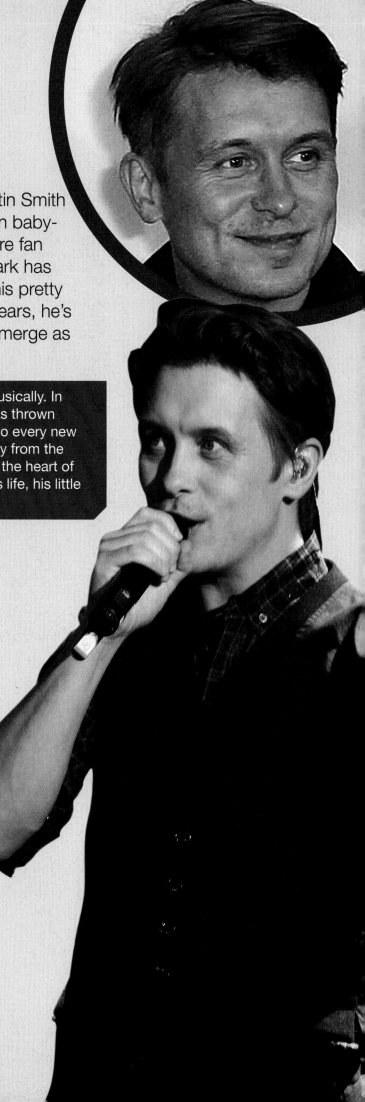

Mark Owen has come a long way since Nigel-Martin Smith first signed him to join Take That. The softly spoken baby-faced star was an instant heartthrob, receiving more fan mail than the rest of the band put together. But Mark has always had so much more to give musically than his pretty boy status would suggest. During the last fifteen years, he's been on a journey – a journey that has seen him emerge as a songwriting force to be reckoned with.

Ever since Take That first split, Mark has kept himself busy musically. In addition to selling over 400,000 records as a solo artist, he has thrown himself into the writing process, pouring his heart and soul into every new composition. Inspiration often comes to him at home, far away from the bright lights – he and his wife Emma share an idyllic retreat in the heart of the Lake District. It also comes from the two other loves of his life, his little boy Elwood Jack and baby girl Willow Rose.

THERE'S ONLY ONE MARK OWEN BECAUSE...

- …it's not about the money. Despite Take That's glittering return to the top of the charts, Mark still regularly tours as a solo artist.

- …he's a beautiful person. In 2002 Mark won Celebrity Big Brother by a landslide, scooping 77% of the vote. His nightly appearances on the UK's TV screens captured the nation's hearts.

- …he's an absolute perfectionist, refusing to let a song go until the melody, instruments, voices and production are all absolutely right. His attitude to touring is just as exacting.

- …he's created a quirky indie style that's all his own.

- …he's brave enough to take each day with the band as it comes, holding no grudges or recriminations, just accepting the gift of Take That and sharing his friendship with the rest of the guys.

MARK'S CREATED A QUIRKY INDIE STYLE THAT'S ALL HIS OWN.

IN 2002 MARK WON
CELEBRITY BIG BROTHER
BY A LANDSLIDE, SCOOPING
77% OF THE VOTE...

Right from the beginning, Take That live gigs have always been something special. With each new tour, the boys have tried to bring their fans something bigger and better – 'Progress Live' was no exception. As well as smashing all previous ticket sales records, around 1.8 million people would finally get to watch Take That perform as a five-piece again. It was quite simply, the biggest tour ever staged in Britain.

The boys spent months planning, designing and rehearsing their set. After watching Gary, Howard, Mark and Jason's amazing 'Circus' show on DVD, Robbie was desperate to create a piece of visual theatre that was just as flamboyant and entertaining. The guys agreed that the shows should represent the band's entire journey – during the gigs Take That would perform as a four-piece and a five-piece, as well as reviving a medley of Robbie's solo hits.

*"Coming from us, this is going to be a big production stadium show, not a stripped back acoustic set. We look forward to coming up with big ideas and for it to be a spectacular." - **Gary***

In the run-up however, nerves began to jangle. Robbie in particular fell prey to an acute stage fright that only got worse as the clock ticked down to show time. The budgets involved were gigantic and the special effects were potentially fraught with risk.

But from the very first number of the very first show, the fans were in raptures. The crowds were enchanted by moving stages, dazzling light displays and captivating dance routines. The music was a joyful celebration of Take That's amazing, evolving sound. The reviews said it all - 'Progress Live' was the pop event of a lifetime.

Progress Live
- The Set List

Take That the four-piece:
Rule The World
Greatest Day
Hold Up A Light
Patience
Shine

Robbie's solo set:
Let Me Entertain You
Rock DJ
Come Undone (Take A Walk
On The Wild Side)
Feel
Angels

Take That reunited:
The Flood
SOS
Underground Machine
Kidz
Pretty Things
Million Love Songs/Babe/
Everything Changes/Back
For Good (piano medley)
Pray
Love Love
Never Forget

The encore:
No Regrets
Relight My Fire
Eight Letters

ON THE ROAD AGAIN

WERE YOU ONE OF THE 1.8 MILLION PEOPLE LUCKY ENOUGH TO SEE THE BAND'S RECORD-BREAKING REUNION SHOW IN 2011? 'PROGRESS' WAS ARGUABLY THE BIGGEST POP TOUR THIS CENTURY, FÊTED WITH GLOWING REVIEWS FROM BOTH FANS AND CRITICS ALIKE. FIND A PEN, THEN TEST YOUR KNOWLEDGE OF THE BAND'S CELEBRATED COMEBACK. CAN YOU NOTCH UP AT LEAST TEN TAKE THAT TRIUMPHS?

QUESTION 1

Where did Take That kick off their 2011 tour?

QUESTION 2

THE BAND OPENED THEIR 'PROGRESS' TOUR DATES BY PERFORMING FIVE SONGS AS A FOUR-PIECE. ROBBIE THEN PLAYED A SELECTION OF HIS SOLO HITS. BUT WHAT WAS THE FIRST SONG THE BAND PLAYED WITH ALL FIVE MEMBERS ON STAGE TOGETHER?

QUESTION 3

Every Take That live show features some amazing set pieces. One of the standout moments from the most recent tour was Jason and Howard's breakdancing contest. What was Robbie doing while his band mates danced it out?

QUESTION 4

SUCH COMPLICATED LIVE GIGS NEED DETAILED REHEARSALS. WHERE DID TAKE THAT PRACTICE FOR THE 'PROGRESS' TOUR?

QUESTION 5

ON JULY 16TH 2011 THE BAND WERE FORCED TO CANCEL THE FIRST EVER CONCERT IN THEIR HISTORY. WHY?

QUESTION 6

Such a big show requires a huge behind-the-scenes team to get the tour on the road and keep producing a knockout show every night. Can you guess, to the nearest ten, how many members were in the 'Progress' tour crew?

QUESTION 7

THE BAND PLAYED TWENTY-SEVEN DATES IN THE UK, INCLUDING AN INCREDIBLE EIGHT SOLD-OUT NIGHTS AT WEMBLEY STADIUM, BEFORE HEADING OUT TO EUROPE FOR SIX MORE SHOWS. IN WHAT CITY DID THEY PLAY THE FINAL DATE?

QUESTION 8

One of the highlights of Take That's set list was their medley of old hits. 'Everything Changes' was seamlessly added to 'Back For Good' to produce a winning update on two classics. With which song was ballad 'A Million Love Songs' joined?

QUESTION 9

The 'Progress' tour featured one of the most complex and memorable stage sets ever created. The part most fans will remember was the fully operational twenty-metre-tall man who joined the band on stage. What did Take That nickname their robot?

QUESTION 10

The penultimate song in the band's set was a new version of their classic cover 'Relight My Fire'. Their original recording reached the top of the charts in 1993 and featured the vocals of Lulu. Which member of the band sang Lulu's part for their 2011 live version?

QUESTION 11

TAKE THAT ALSO TOOK ANOTHER RECORD-BREAKING BAND ON THE ROAD WITH THEM. WHO WERE THE BOYS' SUPPORT ACT?

QUESTION 12

When tickets for the tour were released, the band initially put 1.34 million on sale, holding back the rest for a second round of sales. How long did it take for the huge mega batch of tickets to sell out?

QUESTION 13

A lot of trucks are needed to transport a show as big the 'Progress' tour around Europe. How many trucks were in the Take That tour fleet?

QUESTION 14

During the second round of sales for the tour, demand for tickets was so high that the band was forced to add more dates to cope. How many did they add?

QUESTION 15

WHAT NEW SONG DID THE BAND PICK TO CLOSE THEIR TOUR DATES WITH?

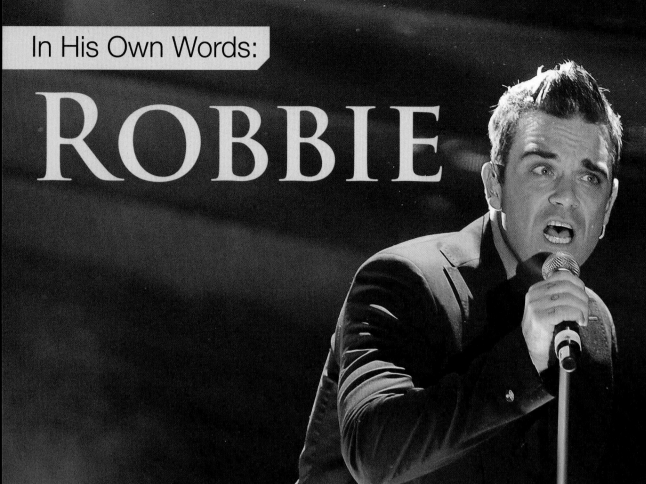

Robbie on...

pre-reunion nerves...

"I was very nervous because there were four of them. I came so close to not going because I had toothache that night and I'd just taken a painkiller. I was quite large as well, and I thought I can't go mumbling, looking like Elvis. I'd said some nasty things about Gaz too. What do I do if I go in, is he harbouring anything? So the missus pushed me through the door."

finally meeting Gary...

"It is one of those situations in life that could be very explosive and could go completely wrong. We had that big chat and the most amazing thing happened at the end of it. We both said sorry to each other and we both meant it and that was all we needed. It just lifted so much off my shoulders that I didn't know was still there."

parking his solo career...

"I'm bored, scared, lonely and I've said everything I want to say in a record. I'm enjoying this too much to want to go back into the Robbie William's band. I'm breaking me up due to musical similarities."

celebrating the reunion...

"The next day I went out and got myself a Take That tattoo to commemorate."

the differences between himself and Gary...

"He's very black and white and I'm several shades of grey. He's a solid man. A well-rounded grown-up. There's still a child in him but he's a grown-up."

moving forward...

"We are a bit older, a bit wiser, I think that our egos have diminished a little bit."

the future...

"The thing is, the door is open to do whatever we want."

his wedding day...

"Ayda looked like the most beautiful girl in the world. To be surrounded by my family and friends and then see Ayda appear looking so radiant was almost too much to take. I am the happiest man alive."

having children...

"Working with kids has made me want to have them. It's on the horizon. I don't know when. I've got a few things that I want to do before that happens."

"WE BOTH SAID SORRY TO EACH OTHER AND WE BOTH MEANT IT"

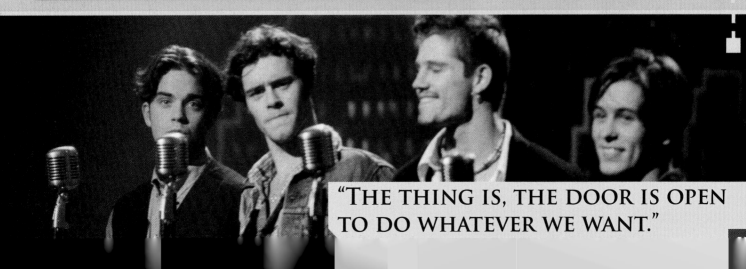

"THE THING IS, THE DOOR IS OPEN TO DO WHATEVER WE WANT."

Behind The Hype:

ROBBIE

More column inches have been written about Robbie Williams than the rest of the band put together. During his record-breaking years as a solo artist, the world has watched him wrestle his demons, move to LA, search for love and finally find happiness in the arms of his wife Ayda Field. The hugely anticipated homecoming of the Take That fold has also given Rob a profound sense of peace and wellbeing.

Robbie is a larger-than-life character in so many ways, but behind the cameras lies a shy guy with a fragile confidence that can easily get bruised. When he's not wowing the crowds as a showman, Robbie lives for the simple things – a game of footie with his mates, walks with the dogs and a cuppa in front of the telly with his wife, Ayda. He's a crazy, complex, perplexing kind of superstar and we wouldn't have him any other way.

THERE'S ONLY ONE ROBBIE WILLIAMS BECAUSE...

- …he's dotty about dogs. When Robbie and Ayda got married, their eight pups walked the bride down the aisle!

- …when he steps on stage, the crowd can't look anywhere else. Robbie's charisma and magnetising star presence are unrivalled in the music business.

- …he's been wowing the fans since the tender age of sixteen. Thanks Rob, for over twenty-one years of unforgettable anthems!

- …he's not afraid to admit to try new hobbies. Since moving to LA, Robbie has got into UFO spotting, claiming to have seen three already!

- …despite selling 57 million albums, breaking a stack of world records and earning wealth beyond his wildest dreams, Robbie is still a lovable lad from Stoke, one who would follow Port Vale FC to the end!

WHEN HE STEPS ON STAGE, THE CROWD CAN'T LOOK ANYWHERE ELSE

HE'S BEEN WOWING THE FANS SINCE THE TENDER AGE OF SIXTEEN. THANKS ROB, FOR OVER TWENTY-ONE YEARS OF UNFORGETTABLE ANTHEMS!

Part 2

The Videos

With each new single release, the lads kept on filming.
What's your favourite Take That reunion video?

Love Love

The arrival of this music video was officially announced on the Take That website on May 27th 2011, debuting the same day. It was directed by Alex Large and Liane Sommers, a British duo working under the name AlexandLiane. AlexandLiane has stellar form, having previously directed vids for Kylie, Cheryl Cole, Mika, the Scissor Sisters and the Ting Tings.

'Love Love' was filmed in a studio-turned-futuristic dome, in West London. The band appeared dressed in sharp tailoring, while a team of dancers performed highly stylised and choreographed moves around them. Clever lighting provided an extra dimension with changing block colours and light-emitting microphone stands. The track also featured in the movie X-men: First Class starring James McAvoy, Kevin Bacon and January Jones. Later, the video was re-released with movie clips seamlessly inter-cut with the original footage.

When We Were Young

This atmospheric black-and-white film was made to accompany the final single from 'Progressed'. It also became the theme song for the remake of the movie The Three Musketeers starring Orlando Bloom and Milla Jovovich.

Filmed across two nights in an empty Wembley Stadium after the band's gig, 'When We Were Young' showed Robbie lying on stage while the last pieces of ticker tape drifted down from the rafters above. Although at times melancholy, with leftover posters and wilting flowers from fans, the video ended on a high note with the lads coming together on stage to take their bows.

Gary spoke of the inspiration for the track itself saying, "The film is visually so rich and beautiful that our main challenge was to then match it musically. We've returned to guitars, real pianos and a conventional song structure to achieve this." He also went on to admit that he and Robbie also thought that the Musketeers reminded them of themselves.

Shame

Robbie and Gary's duet 'Shame' was shot over two days in Chatsworth, Los Angeles and Malibu State Park, the backdrop for cult TV series 'Mash'. Vaughan Arnell was hired as the director, the talent behind Robbie's 'Angels' and 'Rock DJ'.

As the song was about Robbie and Gary's renewed bond, the pair decided that the storyline for the video should give a tongue-in-cheek nod to the bromance film 'Brokeback Mountain'. Scenes included wistful shots of the boys passing each other while grocery shopping and hanging out in the launderette. Later sequences even showed the guys bare-chested, diving from rocks, skimming stones and having heart-to-hearts in the great outdoors. Robbie joked on set
about the concept, laughing that "a casual passer-by might have wondered what was going on . . . but we're just two old friends that have got reacquainted and fancied climbing a mountain . . . with our clothes off!"

Back For Good…

Does anyone know what the future holds? Looking back across the years, not one of us could have predicted the remarkable ups and downs of Take That. It's been a wonderful story, made all the more incredible by you, the fans.

So now we turn to another brand new page. It's a page that we never thought we'd get to and we're so thankful to be here. Are you ready for the next incredible chapter? Hold on tight…!

Love always,

Gary, Mark, Howard, Jason and Robbie xxx

ANSWERS

PAGES 22-23:
WHO SAID THAT?

1. Howard
2. Gary
3. Jason
4. Robbie
5. Mark
6. Gary
7. Howard
8. Robbie
9. Jason
10. Mark
11. Mark
12. Robbie
13. Jason
14. Gary
15. Howard

PAGES 30-31:
LET'S GET LYRICAL

1. Kidz
2. The Flood
3. Man
4. What Do You Want From Me?
5. Affirmation
6. SOS
7. When We Were Young
8. Happy Now
9. Love Love
10. Aliens
11. Pretty Things
12. Wonderful World

13. Underground Machine
14. Eight Letters
15. Wait

PAGES 56-57:
UP CLOSE AND PERSONAL

1. Piano and drums
2. Break-dancing
3. Anthony
4. 5
5. Robbie's father, Peter, ran the club's social club for a while
6. He couldn't stand the auditions
7. Big Brother
8. 'Speak Without Words'
9. The X Factor
10. 57 million
11. Nicola Roberts
12. One
13. Psychology, Biology, History and Sciences
14. 'What Do You Want From Me?'
15. 'Revenge Of The Kidz'

PAGES 64-65:
JOIN THE CHORUS LINE

1. Eight letters
2. Talk about
3. Delicate tale
4. Dance in the rain
5. Heart to talk

6. Die anymore
7. Obviously cunningly, womanly
8. Adored the fabulous
9. Happy now
10. Think I'm in love with you
11. You've loved somebody
12. Bullet To The Head
13. Wanna say
14. Bionic and beyond
15. Fractious, twisted, addicted

PAGES 82-83: ON THE ROAD AGAIN

1. Sunderland's Stadium Of Light

2. 'The Flood'

3. Rapping in an tennis umpire's chair.

4. At an air base in Bedfordshire.

5. Robbie was advised by doctors not to perform after catching a severe stomach infection.

6. 287

7. Munich

8. 'Babe'

9. Om

10. 'Robbie'

11. Pet Shop Boys

12. Just 24 hours

13. 238.

14. 11

15. 'Eight Letters'